Career Exploration

Careers If You Like Problem Solving

James Roland

ReferencePoint Press®

San Diego, CA

© 2020 ReferencePoint Press, Inc.
Printed in the United States

For more information, contact:
ReferencePoint Press, Inc.
PO Box 27779
San Diego, CA 92198
www.ReferencePointPress.com

LIBRARY OF CONGRESS CATALOGING-IN-PUBLICATION DATA

Name: Roland, James, author.
Title: Careers If You Like Problem Solving/By James Roland.
Description: San Diego, CA: ReferencePoint Press, Inc., 2020. | Series:
 Career Exploration | Includes bibliographical references and index. |
 Audience: Grade 9 to 12. |
Identifiers: LCCN 2019011299 (print) | LCCN 2019020613 (ebook) | ISBN
 9781682825907 (eBook) | ISBN 9781682825891 (hardback)
Subjects: LCSH: Technology—Vocational guidance—Juvenile literature. |
 Personnel management—Vocational guidance—Juvenile literature. | Allied
 health personnel—Vocational guidance—Juvenile literature. | Law
 enforcement—Vocational guidance—Juvenile literature. | Vocational
 guidance—Juvenile literature.
Classification: LCC T65.3 (ebook) | LCC T65.3 .R65 2020 (print) | DDC
 331.702—dc23
LC record available at https://lccn.loc.gov/2019011299

Contents

Making a Living Solving Problems

Every day engineers and scientists at the National Aeronautics and Space Administration (NASA) examine one of the greatest challenges humankind has ever faced: how to send astronauts to Mars and bring them home again. It is a mission rife with problems that have to be solved, from designing and building a spacecraft big enough to carry the fuel for the trip there and back to making sure there is enough food, water, and oxygen for everyone on board.

Of the myriad other challenging problems facing the space program, one has to do with aerobraking, the procedure in which a spacecraft uses friction from the thin Martian atmosphere to slow down and settle safely into the planet's orbit so that it can deploy a landing craft to the surface. "One of the problems of getting a spacecraft to another planet is that we first have to get it out of Earth's orbit," explains Walter Engelund with NASA's Langley Research Center. "So we have to speed it up to a high enough velocity to break free of the Earth's gravity field. Then, when the spacecraft gets to its destination planet, it has to slow down enough so that it is 'captured' into orbit around that planet's gravity field."[1] Once on the planet's surface, scientists and explorers need to be able to survive on another planet for the first time.

Searching for Solutions on the Job

People like Engelund are born problem solvers. They look at the monumental task of sending a spacecraft millions of miles to a planet with an unbreathable atmosphere and an unstable surface as a fascinating puzzle—a mystery in need of a solution.

Although not every occupation's concerns stretch across the solar system, just about every job entails some degree of problem solving. There are many career options in which finding solutions to challenges is mostly what the job is all about. Mechanics who open car hoods all day long to figure out what's wrong with the engine are problem solvers. Judges listening to both sides in a lawsuit are problem solvers.

Jobs that require a lot of problem solving are not for everyone. Relatively few people are cut out to be emergency room doctors or homicide detectives, for example. But for the people who make a career of finding solutions, problems are welcome challenges. These individuals enjoy the investigation and exploration involved in discovering and defining the problem. They draw satisfaction in coming up with a solution, relying on their creativity, experience, and knowledge.

Solving problems all day (or all night) long can be stressful, even for the people who willingly take on such challenges. At the end of a day spent under sinks and crawling through basements or attics, plumbers are ready to stretch out and relax. After a long shift responding to medical emergencies, paramedics need to find ways to de-stress and let go of some of the day's grim memories.

And yet, a paramedic who saves a life or a manager who figures out a solution to an ongoing personnel problem at the office can look back on the day satisfied that his or her skills led to the best possible outcome. It is often that reward that keeps people in problem-solving jobs coming back day after day ready for a new challenge.

The financial rewards of a problem-solving job vary considerably. Income is often tied to a person's education, experience, and the responsibility of the job. Where you live and work and the size and type of the organization that employs you also affect how much you make.

Explore the Careers That Interest You Now

If the idea of working to solve problems appeals to you, think about where your interests and abilities lie. If you enjoy science and math, then being an engineer may satisfy that problem-solving urge. If biology and health care hold your interests, then consider any of the hundreds of different jobs in the life sciences. Computer skills can lead to careers in tech support or cybersecurity—both of which are all about solving and preventing problems.

Try to talk with people who do the jobs that interest you and ask about their education and experience. Your school's guidance counselor may have material to read and tests you can take that can help shape your career planning.

You may be one of the scientists or engineers who help get astronauts to Mars and back. Or you may be the nurse who takes care of babies who need medical care right after they're born. Doing a job in which you solve problems means you're helping others. You're tackling those challenges so everyone else has fewer problems of their own to solve.

Biomedical Engineer

A Few Facts

Number of Jobs
21,300 in 2016

Median Salary
$88,040

Minimum Educational Requirements
Bachelor's degree, although some jobs require advanced degrees

Personal Qualities
Analytical; creative; an interest in engineering and medicine; strong in math and science; good communication skills

Work Settings
Laboratories; universities; hospitals; research facilities of companies or medical institutions

Future Job Outlook
7 percent growth through 2026

What Does a Biomedical Engineer Do?

All types of engineers are problem solvers. They size up a problem and design and build a solution. Biomedical engineers, also known as bioengineers, provide engineering solutions to problems with the body's organ systems. For example, our veins and arteries occasionally have problems with blockages. A stent is a tiny mesh tube that can be inserted into a blood vessel at the site of a blockage to improve blood flow. Biomedical engineers invented stents and continue to work on ways to make them more effective and safer for the patients who need them.

Sometimes the tissue lining a blood vessel wall can start to grow around the stent, narrowing the vein or artery again. This is called restenosis, and it can cause serious circulation complications if it's not caught early. To help solve this problem, biomedical engineers are developing newer stents equipped with sensors that can determine if a clogged artery is starting to narrow again and may lead to a heart attack. "The essence of the technology is its unique ability to provide early warning of re-narrowing, to address it before it becomes severe leading to heart attack," says Kenichi Takahata, an associate professor in the Department of Electrical and Computer Engineering at the University of British Columbia. "Allowing for continuous monitoring, it can lower the cost for diagnosis as well."[2]

The development of stents, artificial heart valves, prosthetic limbs, dental implants, surgical instruments, and other devices and products to assist doctors and other health care professionals in treating their patients is known as medical device engineering—one of several biomedical engineering specialties.

Other specialties include clinical engineering, medical imaging, and tissue engineering. Whereas device engineering focuses more on handheld tools or items that are implanted in or fitted to a patient, clinical engineering solves problems associated with the storage and sharing of increasingly large amounts of patient data or managing or operating continuously more sophisticated equipment. Surgical robotics and hybrid rooms used for both open-heart operations and less invasive catheter procedures are examples of clinical engineering. A clinical engineer often serves as the technology manager for a hospital's medical equipment systems. Clinical engineers may be responsible for training employees on new equipment and for evaluating new equipment and systems.

The term *medical imaging* refers to diagnostic screenings such as X-rays, computed tomography scans, and other equipment used to look inside the body. A bioengineer in this field might focus on inventing new equipment or perfecting existing imaging technology. In tissue engineering, bioengineers create or improve artificial tissue that is used to create new organs, such as synthetic skin and bladders.

To help solve the problem of excessive scarring and slow healing associated with skin grafts for burn victims, Ioannis Yannas, an engineering professor at the Massachusetts Institute of Technology, helped develop artificial skin using collagen and tissue compounds from animal tendons and cartilage. The material is grafted onto the damaged skin of burn victims, triggering the growth of new skin tissue in areas that would otherwise have been considered dead. "For years, we did not understand the impact that this discovery would have," Yannas says, admitting that he and other researchers underestimated the degree to which the artificial skin was actually stimulating the growth of new, human skin cells. "We simply thought it was a new treatment for burn victims. Eventually, it became clear that we were regenerating a new organ."[3]

Bioengineers are also at the forefront of the development of new vaccines and medicines to conquer incurable diseases or medical conditions that need more effective and safer treatments. The creation and improvement of medications, artificial organs, and other treatments is sometimes referred to as therapeutic bioengineering.

A Typical Workday

The average workday for a biomedical engineer depends on whether he or she is focused more on research, operating high-tech equipment in a hospital, or working on the actual design and construction of new products. Researchers may also be college professors, who spend some days in a classroom teaching the next generation of engineers while spending other days in a lab.

Chae-Ok Yun of South Korea is one of those bioengineers who is both a professor and a researcher. Much of her research has been in developing new ways to manipulate a patient's genes to help treat cancer. She explains that,

> as a scientist and a professor, my typical day is focused on teaching the younger generation of engineering students and expanding on my own research. I teach both undergraduate and graduate students in bioengineering as well as guide the students at my lab, aiming to help them improve their research and methodology skills, and their general understanding of bioengineering. Concurrently, I communicate with different researchers and industrial leaders to perform innovative and collaborative research and to pioneer new technological advancements for the benefit of cancer patients. I hope to one day be able to aid these people in their battles with this illness. The most satisfactory aspect of my role is the notion that my research and teaching will one day aid the future generation of engineers, fulfill their potential and dreams in this field and ultimately bring societal progress.[4]

Research can mean developing computer models for the devices they're working on or testing their creations on three-dimensional apparatuses like a phantom brain model, which is an artificial brain designed to respond to stimuli just as a human brain would. Researchers at the University of Pittsburgh, for example, spent countless hours developing an alternative treatment for deep brain stimulation, in which mild electrical charges are delivered at targeted parts of the brain affected by conditions such as Parkinson's disease. Researchers working with Professor Takashi D.Y. Kozai developed a system that uses light energy rather than an electrical wire to stimulate brain tissue. The wire can cause scarring or other injury to the brain. "We hope to reduce some of the damage by replacing this large cable with long wavelength light and an ultrasmall, untethered electrode,"[5] says Kozai.

Education and Training

Although an interest in science and math is key for any type of aspiring engineer, biomedical engineering requires a curiosity and knowledge specifically related to life sciences, such as biology, anatomy, and biochemistry.

Biomedical engineers often earn a bachelor's degree in biomedical engineering, though some people enter the field having studied other aspects of engineering, such as materials engineering, chemical engineering, and electrical or computer engineering. Because so many diagnostic tools are computer based, a strong background in digital technology can lead to a career as a bioengineer and specifically a clinical engineer. Most supervisory or research jobs may require a master's degree or a doctorate.

A doctorate in biomedical engineering isn't required for most entry-level jobs in the field. Many bioengineers have master's degrees. People who seek a doctoral degree often focus on research and teaching at the university level or simply want to further their education and training to advance in more managerial roles. Working as any type of engineer also requires a professional engineer license, which is obtained through a combination of education, work experience, and passing professional exams.

Skills and Personality

Biomedical engineers often spend many hours with an eye staring through a microscope or at a computer developing models of body parts and systems. But being able to communicate with others, especially regarding complex ideas, is an essential trait for bioengineers.

Patience and a willingness to view failures and setbacks as helpful learning opportunities is also crucial, explains bioengineer Shivani Ludwig, the innovation development manager at Xinova, a Seattle-based tech company involved in many fields, including medicine. "One of the biggest hurdles to innovation is getting the problem right," she says. "So much time and effort is often spent on solving the wrong problem. It's just as challenging, if not more, to understand the true root of a problem. In fact, one of the most surprising things about working in innovation is that the 'failed' ideas help us ask the right questions to zero in on the problem we need to solve."[6]

Working Conditions

Biomedical engineers usually work indoors in offices, laboratories, manufacturing plants, hospitals, and clinics. For example, an engineer specializing in robotic surgery may spend a lot of time in operating rooms monitoring how the equipment is working or learning more about what surgeons need when doing complicated procedures.

Bioengineers often work with other engineers and researchers as well as with health care providers, such as physicians, nurses, and physical therapists. Bioengineers can also be consultants hired by medical device companies or other organizations to evaluate their products or give input into products or ideas in development. Michaelina Dupnik is a bioengineer with the Massachusetts-based consulting firm Optimum Technologies. "We're hired by various companies to give our optical expertise for their products, whether it is a 3D camera system for a robotic surgeon or a novel surgical technique for a breakthrough procedure to cure macular degeneration," she says. "Working for a consulting company is great because you are working on something different every day and there's never a dull moment."[7]

Employers and Pay

Biomedical engineers are usually employed at universities, hospitals and other medical institutions, and companies that develop and manufacture medical devices and other health-related tech, such as advanced imaging systems or virtual organs used to train surgeons. Bioengineers working in the private sector tend to make more than those working in a government or academic setting.

With a median salary of about $88,000, biomedical engineers can expect to make anywhere from $52,000 to nearly $143,000. Bioengineers in the private sector developing new medical equipment, devices, and medications tend to make the most money, while those teaching and doing research at colleges and universities usually make less.

What Is the Future Outlook for Biomedical Engineers?

Biomedical engineering is definitely a growth field, with an estimated 7 percent growth expected through 2026, according to the Bureau of Labor Statistics. As the nation's population ages and the need for innovative health care solutions grows, biomedical engineers will be in high demand.

Find Out More

Cleveland Clinic Department of Biomedical Engineering
Lerner Research Institute
9500 Euclid Ave.
Cleveland, OH 44195
website: www.lerner.ccf.org/bme

The Cleveland Clinic isn't just a world-renowned hospital. It's also where medical innovations are being made every year, from new heart devices to treatments involving a patient's own genes. Learn about the leading programs in biomedical engineering and see what the professionals are working on in labs today that will be in a doctor's hands tomorrow.

Michigan Tech Department of Biomedical Engineering
309 Minerals & Materials Engineering Bldg.
1400 Townsend Dr.
Houghton, MI 49931
website: www.mtu.edu/biomedical

Learn about what biomedical engineering is, what biomedical engineers do every day, and what kind of education is needed for this career. There's also information about salaries and about some of the fascinating research that college students are doing right now.

Purdue School of Engineering and Technology
799 W. Michigan St.
Indianapolis, IN 46202
website: www.engr.iupui.edu

If you're wondering about a career in biomedical engineering, this site will help answer any questions. Its web page titled "Is Biomedical Engineering Right for Me?" includes a lot of information about the courses you'll take and the many kinds of jobs you can pursue once you're out of college.

Human Resources Manager

What Does a Human Resources Manager Do?

A human resources (HR) manager oversees most aspects of employment, such as recruiting and hiring employees, training, payroll, health insurance and other benefits, complying with labor laws, performance management and job evaluations, and helping create the work environment envisioned by the owners or upper management of the organization.

An HR manager often serves as a link between employees and management. A company of any size is bound to have employees who, at some point, experience conflict with a manager or colleague. A part of an HR manager's responsibilities is to help solve whatever problems a worker is having with a coworker or his or her supervisor. Solving such problems usually means asking the right questions of the people involved, listening carefully, and assessing the situation. Sometimes an HR manager facilitates communication between the parties or proposes changes in the workplace to satisfy everyone involved. "It's really gratifying to see employees go from being frustrated because they're having a problem with their manager to feeling productive and appreciated,"[8] says Lynda Spiegel, an HR manager and certified life coach.

A Typical Workday

An HR manager's workday depends largely on the size of the department and the nature of the company or organization. A small company or nonprofit organization may have only a few people in HR, meaning the manager is often hands-on with most responsibilities of the department. A large HR department means the manager can delegate more work to assistants and specialists in certain areas, such as recruiting or benefits.

Many HR managers agree that no two days are alike. And for many of them, that's part of the appeal of the job. "I like the fact that no day is ever the same and that I truly learn constantly,"[9] says Jon Thurmond, the regional HR manager with Team Fishel, a large construction firm based in Florida.

An HR manager might spend the morning welcoming new employees and in the afternoon help senior managers develop a plan to reorganize a department or negotiate health benefits with an insurance provider. HR manager Lisa Rosendahl describes her job:

> On any given day, I could be developing our strategic workforce succession plan, meeting with an employee who has a question about her pay, reviewing a proposed disciplinary action or a grievance response, developing a position description for a new HR position, responding to a suspense from our network office, listening to a conference call about changes in our hiring process, gathering market data for nurse salary, or reviewing a request for reasonable accommodation. . . . I like the variety of human resource work. I am an HR generalist so I touch all areas of human resources. There are opportunities to specialize in a specific area such as recruitment, benefits, employee relations or labor relations and it depends on your interests.[10]

Education and Training

Many university business schools offer undergraduate degrees in HR or HR management. Some people further focus their business education with a master of business administration degree with a concentration in HR. Internships with HR departments in the public or private sectors can help lead to entry-level jobs in the field.

Some HR managers start out on one career path only to be drawn by the challenges and rewards of helping a business with its employee and administrative problems. "I started my career as a teacher and 'fell' into HR," says Thurmond. "Since then, I've worked in several industries and with companies from 200 to 20,000 employees."[11] As a result of these career changes, the educational backgrounds of HR managers tend to vary considerably. Typically, an education in business or a business-related field, such as management or accounting, can be especially helpful. However, for students already planning on an HR career, a bachelor's degree in HR management is a good option.

An undergraduate degree can help you get started in HR. You may work as an HR assistant, specialist, or generalist. These positions report to an HR manager and provide valuable experience in learning how an HR department operates. An HR specialist focuses on a specific area, such as recruiting or risk management, and a generalist can work in all aspects of HR. Larger organizations can afford to have specialists who develop a greater knowledge and experience level in a given discipline.

Smaller organizations need HR generalists to handle just about anything that involves the department—payroll, benefits, organizational development, and more.

Generally, having a master's degree is necessary to become an HR manager. It's not uncommon for an HR specialist to earn a master's degree while working. Some employers pay to have their prospective managers earn an advanced degree, with the hope that the education will benefit the company. "Principles and concepts learned during any graduate program expose the HR professional to viewpoints he or she may not have been exposed to previously,"[12] says Nancy Woolever, the director of academic initiatives at the Society for Human Resource Management.

In addition to advanced degrees, HR managers often earn the professional human resources certification and the certified employment benefits specialist certification. Earning these certifications from the Human Resources Certification Institute is done through a combination of work experience and classes.

Skills and Personality

Because HR involves everyone employed at a particular company or organization, it's helpful for HR managers to be comfortable interacting with all types of people. They need to be outgoing and willing to listen to all sides if there is a dispute among employees or between an employee and a supervisor.

The key to being an effective problem solver is to help everyone involved in a conflict remember that they are all on the same side. Pamela Potts is an HR manager for a company that provides financial, human resources, and data management services to other businesses. "HR can feel the pressure of high stakes like anyone else," Potts says. "Start by remembering you are the solution, not the problem. Then get the parties in conflict to agree on a common goal. If they can agree that they are all working toward the same goal and are willing to be open to new solutions, then the conversation becomes about how to best reach the goal rather than parties staking out positions."[13]

But HR is more than just interacting with people. It also requires a skill with numbers because the HR department handles salaries, benefits, and other administrative aspects of a business. HR managers make sure salaries and bonuses are within an organization's budget. They also work with other department heads to plan future budgets that must consider raises, cost-of-living adjustments, restructuring, and other payroll-related demands. They also try to find the best health insurance for their employees, which will satisfy economic needs while also providing comprehensive coverage.

Working Conditions

An HR manager usually works indoors in an office. A manager with a company that has many offices or locations may need to travel often to meet with employees in their workplaces. Because the HR manager must be a familiar face to all employees, he or she at times will meet with employees where they work: on the factory floor, reception area, cafeteria, or in other areas where employees work and gather.

Generally, an HR manager works during regular business hours. Travel to conferences or to meet with contractors who work with the company may also be necessary.

Employers and Pay

HR managers work in almost every industry. They are employed by banks, hospitals, restaurant chains, department stores, insurance companies, and government agencies. The job is typically considered part of a company's upper management team, often commanding a six-figure salary. Larger companies, which place more responsibility in the hands of an HR manager, may pay up to about $140,000, while local governments and nonprofit organizations often pay closer to $100,000, as they often have fewer employees and demands on the HR department. For-profit companies also tend to pay their managers more than nonprofit groups. And because most organizations have HR departments, you can enter the field and gain experience with one employer and move up in your career by changing employers if there is little advancement opportunity where you currently work. HR, like accounting and a few other business-related fields, means there is opportunity in all parts of the country and in almost any industry.

What Is the Future Outlook for Human Resources Managers?

A 9 percent job growth rate is likely for the HR manager position through 2026, according to the Bureau of Labor Statistics. As the number of start-ups increases and more companies, nonprofit organizations, and other employers emerge, HR managers will be needed to help them find and keep good employees and help create and maintain an efficient and appealing work environment.

During times when the economy is growing and there is greater competition for hiring new employees, an effective HR manager who oversees a training program that gets new employees trained

A Dynamic Department

"My misconception of HR when first presented with the opportunity in the interview was HR as a bunch of tired people in a back room processing pay raises. So, needless to say, I begrudgingly went to observe HR in action. I was pleasantly surprised when I observed a dynamic, interactive HR department involved with employees, managers, leaders and union officials across the facility leading teams, developing programs, solving problems and making a difference. Yes, pay raises were processed but they were automated and there was no tucking HR away in a back room in this organization."

—Lisa Rosendahl, HR manager

Quoted in JobShadow.com, "Interview with a Human Resources Director." http://jobshadow.com.

and productive quickly is a real asset to a company. During economic downturns, when companies are downsizing or restructuring, HR managers play a key role in helping employees learn new responsibilities. And as issues such as health insurance become more complex, it helps any organization to have an HR manager comfortable with changing trends and regulations. Employers generally are becoming more aware of issues such as work-life balance and how stress can affect an employee's health and job performance. To that end, organizations are beefing up HR departments and tasking them with projects like workplace wellness programs that promote exercise and other healthy lifestyle changes.

Find Out More

HumanResourcesEDU.org
website: www.humanresourcesedu.org

This site includes information about undergraduate and graduate degree programs in human resources, profiles of various HR jobs, such as HR manager and hiring manager, and how to find a college or university that has what you need.

Human Resources MBA
website: www.humanresourcesmba.net

This site lists ten very different but very interesting types of HR jobs, such as international human resources professional and an HR entrepreneur. Read the article "10 Best Careers for Human Resources Professionals" to learn about where an HR career can lead and see if one of these paths makes sense for you.

Society for Human Resource Management (SHRM)
website: www.shrm.org

The SHRM certifies HR specialists and managers and offers training opportunities as well as news and other information about the profession. You'll learn about the education and training needed to advance in HR and what HR jobs are like in various industries.

Tech Support Specialist

A Few Facts

Number of Jobs
835,300

Median Salary
$52,810 in 2016

Minimum Educational Requirements
Associate's degree or bachelor's degree; certifications in various computer systems

Personal Qualities
High-level computer skills; patience; analytical and problem-solving skills; empathy; good communication skills

Work Settings
Almost exclusively indoors, in settings such as a call support center or at the site of an employer working directly on computers, servers, and other technology

Future Job Outlook
11 percent growth through 2026

What Does a Tech Support Specialist Do?

From the fisheries of New England to the farms of Iowa to California's Silicon Valley itself, there are few industries in which employees do not rely on computers and the Internet for at least part of their work. In addition, a majority of Americans rely on computer technology at home. A Pew Research Center study found that about 80 percent of US households have at least one smartphone or personal computer.

And when those individual devices or massive computer systems have problems, who is there to solve them? Tech support specialists are the experts on the other end of the phone line, answering questions about personal computers and companywide computing systems. They are the men and women who show up at businesses, schools, government offices, and everywhere else people need computer and Internet assistance to get back to work.

They install, configure, and update hardware and software. This can mean confronting a host of problems, such as insufficient network bandwidth, making sure a new system is compatible with existing equipment and software programs, doing the work within budget constraints, and troubleshooting setup errors or freezes during an installation or upgrade.

Tech support specialists are typically called upon to help solve problems with existing systems. Whether the problems are due to power surges, aging equipment, poor Internet connectivity, viruses and hacking, user errors, or any other reasons, tech support specialists must be able to analyze the root causes of the problem and implement solutions quickly and thoroughly.

Tech support specialists are also known as help desk technicians, computer support specialists, operations analysts, and problem managers. No matter the title, their main job is to act as a troubleshooter, solving problems as they arise and also keeping a company's computers and network working smoothly. Sometimes they work with a network engineer, who is ultimately responsible for setting up and maintaining a company's local and wide-area computer network.

Still, much of the job involves listening to an end user's concerns and questions and then applying one's know-how to reach the best solution. "We need to make sure we know how to diagnose their issues and do it quickly," says Guido Diaz, a senior computer support specialist at Florida International University. "Customer relations and troubleshooting are very important."[14]

A Typical Workday

A tech support specialist who works at an information technology (IT) help desk spends much of the day answering calls and helping either customers or fellow employees with a wide range of questions and problems. "A typical day begins with logging in and setting up all of my programs for the day," says Mai Yia Vue, a help desk specialist for U.S. Bank in Minneapolis. She adds,

> As an IT help desk specialist, I am responsible for the support of numerous systems. I always have at least 10 different applications open. Once I'm set up, I'm assigned to take either calls or chats. Both are set up in a way that I'm "on-call" for incoming calls or chats. The work I do daily is pretty broad. Some examples include password resets, how-to's, break/fix, uninstall/reinstalls, or escalations for larger issues as needed.[15]

A tech support specialist who works as part of his or her employer's IT department can spend much of the day traveling from office to office. The problems that need solving can range from an employee whose computer has frozen up to helping someone update his or her operating system or connect to the office wireless network.

Tech support specialists also work on an organization's computer systems, taking care of the servers that store the company's information and connect individual devices to the network. These specialists are responsible for managing technological resources and testing existing equipment and software as well as evaluating technology that the organization might buy.

Many tech support specialists set up and run training sessions for their colleagues on a variety of issues, such as using a new operating system or email program. Training programs may involve working with small groups of employees or one-on-one sessions with managers to help empower them to deal with smaller tech problems as they arise in a particular department.

Education and Training

Because the key to success as a tech support specialist is extensive and current computer knowledge, the formal education requirements are less rigid in this field than in some others. An associate's degree in computer technical support or a related field is often enough to land a job. Although an extensive academic background may not be necessary, you do need a solid understanding of computers and networks to get hired and keep a job. Mihai Stanciu, a student at Brookhaven College in Texas, is studying computer science with plans to get into tech support. "This is a field where you have to practice. You have to understand how the commands work and how they all connect and work together—which actually goes into trouble shooting," he says. "If you don't understand how things work, you'll be going around in circles. That's why we spend so much time reviewing."[16]

As with most careers, though, advancing into managerial roles often demands more education, such as a bachelor's degree. Becoming certified in certain computer skills is often necessary for specific jobs. A common starter certification is called CompTIA A+. Some tech companies, such as Microsoft and Cisco, also offer training and certifications for their products. Jobs that often need computer certification include database manager, help desk technician, and web developer.

Once you've started your career, ongoing training is necessary to keep up with new programs, applications, and other changes in technology, explains Vue. "Working in a support center that handles several different applications can be overwhelming," she says. "It took time to nail them all down. The learning is continuous. As systems in the company change, new things appear. It's challenging to keep up."[17]

Skills and Personality

A tech support specialist must have highly developed computer skills and a curiosity to keep learning more about technology as new developments emerge. Being detail oriented is vital for success in this job because many computer problems are the result of small program errors that might be overlooked by others. Writing computer code, for example, demands meticulous attention to details. And because a tech support specialist is often dealing with an exasperated consumer or coworker, being a patient, sympathetic listener is quite helpful. A thick skin is also especially helpful because you may bear the brunt of a customer's frustration. It also helps to have a natural desire to help people because the very nature of the job is to play a support role.

Other necessary skills include being a good communicator. Much of the problem-solving part of the job is being able to discover the problem and then explain the solution to the person or people who need help. Tech support specialists involved with training must also be able to take very technical language and concepts and present them in layman's terms to coworkers.

Working Conditions

Tech support specialists employed at call centers often work in a busy room full of cubicles. They answer phone calls from customers and work at computers, surrounded by many other tech support specialists. They may work a normal nine-to-five schedule, or they may work a different eight-hour shift if their employer maintains a twenty-four-hour-a-day tech support operation.

Tech support consultants or other IT specialists who visit job sites are sometimes required to crawl under or behind desks and squeeze into closets or other tight spaces that hold servers and other equipment. They may need to run cables through ceilings or do other tasks that demand a certain amount of agility and physical strength.

Employers and Pay

Tech support specialists work for software developers, computer manufacturers, Internet service providers, and other companies that provide customer support for tech-related products. For example, cable television companies have large teams of specialists to help customers restore a lost connection or resolve a poor-quality signal. Companies like banks, hospitals, universities, and other organizations have tech support specialists on staff to help consumers access their information or pay bills. An organization's IT support staff may be called upon to fix problems like jammed printers or to find and restore documents that have been accidentally deleted.

The average salary for this work is $52,810. Software publishers often pay higher than other companies, while computer support specialists who work for schools and training centers usually make less. Some IT consultants charge by the hour, so they can make considerably more or less depending on what they charge and how much they work. Ambitious tech support specialists can get special training and become project managers, helping set up or renovate a company's computer networks.

What Is the Future Outlook for Tech Support Specialists?

Nearly half of the world's population—about 3.5 billion people—has Internet access, and that number is growing. So, given the increasing prevalence of smartphones and other computer-related technologies in use today, it makes sense that the demand for skilled tech support specialists will only grow in the years ahead.

Likewise, the rise of artificial intelligence and other breakthroughs in automation will also spur the need for more tech support specialists every year. But the demand will be for individuals who not only have cutting-edge computer skills but plenty of customer service skills, too, says John Reed, senior executive director of a technology staffing company. As Reed explains,

> Tomorrow's employers will be looking for a complex mix of skills and attributes in the technical support personnel they hire. This can include everything from the customer service mindset to industry knowledge to the ability to think creatively. That's a tall order. The research we've conducted over the past two years shows that many businesses are having ongoing difficulty finding skilled talent for many current positions in IT. As technology continues to evolve, it will only become more challenging to find professionals who possess the right mix of knowledge, experience, and attributes necessary to assume emerging roles and responsibilities in technical support.[18]

Find Out More

Computer Science Zone
website: www.computersciencezone.org

On this computer science website, the article titled "The 50 Highest Paying Jobs in Computer Science" lists fifty well-paying jobs, including several in the tech support field. Read detailed job descriptions and learn what degrees will help get you those jobs, along with salary ranges for each position.

ECPI Blog
website: www.ecpi.edu/blog

This blog includes the post "What Does a Computer Network Support Specialist Do?" You can learn about tech support specialists and how to advance into other career fields. There's also information about median salaries for the various types of tech support specialists.

Urban Technology Project
website: https://utp-philly.org/programs/computer-support
-specialists/meet-the-computer-support-specialists

On this website, you can read the profiles of young people who became computer support specialists. Find out what motivated them to pursue this job and what classes and training they took to prepare for this career path.

Clinical Psychologist

What Does a Clinical Psychologist Do?

Of all the careers for people who like to solve problems, a clinical psychologist is unique because the job is largely about helping others learn how to solve their own problems. These psychologists diagnose and treat people with mental disorders as well as individuals who are facing any type of distress. They do all this by observing people, interpreting their words and actions, and helping them learn strategies to better cope with the challenges in their lives. A clinical psychologist's job is to help clients think and act in ways that are healthier and that will help them reach certain goals. Clinical psychologists identify their clients' problems through interviews, tests, and observations of how they act and the words they choose when describing themselves and the challenges in their lives. They then share what they have learned and observed with their clients to come up with a treatment plan.

The list of issues that clinical psychologists encounter with their clients is seemingly endless. The types of conditions they treat include depression and anxiety, learning difficulties, behavioral problems, and emotional challenges related to abuse, grieving, aging, and other life-changing circumstances. Clients often see clinical psychologists when they know something is wrong, but they can't quite explain or understand the problem. Others come to psychologists knowing their challenges but needing help in finding a solution. Once a psychological, behavioral, or emotional problem has been identified, the psychologist and client will come up with goals for treatment and then a program to achieve those goals. Sometimes a clinical psychologist will refer a client to a psychiatrist, who, as a medical doctor, is qualified to prescribe medications. Psychiatrists tend to see patients with a range of conditions that require medication, including bipolar disorder, schizophrenia, and even attention-deficit/hyperactivity disorder.

Ryan Howes, a clinical psychologist in California, explains that being a psychologist means joining clients on their journeys to overcome the problems and challenges in their lives. It's a role that good psychologists cherish and take quite seriously. "I essentially earn my living watching stories of strength and perseverance unfold before me," Howes adds. "I get to join them and help them along the way as we share the obstacles and successes together. I'm honored."[19]

A Typical Workday

Clinical psychologists often start out by reviewing the files of the people they will see that day, making notes of what might be covered during those sessions. One by one, clients will spend an hour or so talking with the psychologist. If it's the person's first session, the psychologist may ask a lot of questions about the individual's life and why he or she is seeking therapy. Clients who have been in therapy for a longer time will talk about what's been happening since the last appointment and how they have been applying some of the strategies learned in previous sessions.

Part of the workday may also include research into a problem facing one of their clients. Online resources and books can help, but so, too, can consultations with colleagues who may have expertise in treating a particular condition. Clinical psychologists also need to keep up with new research and often attend conferences to further their knowledge. Although a session may be a one-on-one experience, clinical psychologists often sit down with clients after much collaboration with others.

A clinical psychologist may work with a client's primary care physician if, for example, the client has heart disease that may have triggered the onset of depression. If a client has an eating disorder, a psychologist may consult with a nutritionist. With parental permission, a psychologist treating a child may talk with teachers or school officials about behavior or learning issues. A psychologist may also consult with a social worker to help a client whose mental or emotional challenges are interfering with his or her ability to find steady work or pay the bills on time. The problems that a clinical psychologist helps solve often extend into the day-to-day responsibilities of a client and the client's family.

Although talk-based therapy is the most common treatment employed by clinical psychologists, there are many others. Art therapy, for example, allows clients to draw, paint, use clay, assemble collages or use other art materials to express thoughts and feelings. Music and dance therapies take a similar approach by finding ways other than words to express oneself. Clinical psychologists might also employ role play, meditation, or even group interaction in their treatments.

No matter what special approach a psychologist uses, the job can be mentally and physically draining. Clinical psychologist Joseph Luciani says that although the work is incredibly rewarding, it requires therapists to take care of themselves:

> It can be grueling to see 8, 9, or 10 clients a day. In order to be there for every person who sits in front of you expecting your full attention and dedication, you must take care of your physical health. I start my day at 11:00 a.m. I do this in order to jog every morning, take a yoga class once a week and do some meditation. Just as the yoga postures were designed to enhance the ability to sit quietly and meditate for long hours, so too must a psychologist prepare him or herself for the long periods of sitting while maintaining optimum alertness.[20]

Education and Training

Most clinical psychologists start by earning a bachelor's degree in psychology. That's usually followed by a master's degree in clinical psychology or a more specialized degree in an area such as child and adolescent psychology. But to have your own psychology practice, you must earn a doctoral degree, usually a doctor of psychology or a doctor of philosophy. Most states require a doctoral degree to work as a clinical psychologist.

At the start of a career, a clinical psychologist usually completes a one- to two-year internship with a practicing psychologist. To practice psychology, you must also become licensed by the state in which you work. In addition to having the educational background, a clinical psychologist must accrue more than one thousand hours of clinical work experience (some states require

A clinical psychologist listens as a young woman explains what is troubling her. Clinical psychologists help clients identify problems that are negatively affecting their lives and help them find ways to address those problems.

more hours). The license must be renewed periodically, and to do so you must take continuing education courses to keep current with changing laws and trends in clinical psychology.

Skills and Personality

Because being a psychologist is literally a job in which you spend all day working on solutions to other people's problems, perhaps the most important trait to have is a desire to help others. "I had always, throughout my life, been intuitively inclined to help people with problems," says Luciani. "Understanding human nature always seemed natural to me. It was this intuition that always made psychological problems seem transparent."[21]

Empathy is important because a psychologist needs to be able to understand a patient's emotional struggles. Empathy is simply the ability to put yourself in another person's situation to truly understand and share that person's feelings and experiences.

Organizational skills and the ability to multitask are also essential. Clinical psychologists must keep track of multiple clients along their individual journeys in order to provide them with the right kind of care. Likewise, organization is important if you also do research or run your own practice and have to take care of business matters along with client care.

Working Conditions

Most clinical psychologists work in an office or a clinical setting, such as a hospital or mental health treatment facility. Because psychologists may see students after school or adults after work, they often work later hours during the week or may work on weekends.

Employers and Pay

A clinical psychologist might have his or her own office or be part of a large practice of mental health professionals. Hospitals and clinics often have psychologists and counselors on staff. Large educational institutions such as universities might employ clinical psychologists to treat students. The median salary for clinical psychologists is $77,030, although that figure can vary greatly depending on years of experience and whether a psychologist is part of a large group practice or is an independent practitioner. A clinical psychologist working in a large, thriving practice could make more than $90,000 a year. Schools and outpatient care centers pay closer to the median salary.

What Is the Future Outlook for Clinical Psychologists?

The demand for clinical psychologists isn't likely to subside, especially as the US population ages. "The demand for mental health services is expected to rise as large cohorts of middle-aged individuals—who tend to be more accepting of mental health services than the current generation of older people—move into old age," says Deborah DiGilio, the director of the American Psychological Association's Office on Aging. "Plus, there's evidence that two-thirds of older adults with a mental disorder do not receive needed services."[22]

One of the biggest industry shifts occurring now—and one that is likely to grow in the years ahead—concerns the use of technology. The standard model of a patient arriving at a clinical psychologist's office for a session and then returning a week later may become less common. The convenience of online sessions and the ability of a psychologist to check in with a client between visits via text messaging or other platforms is already taking hold. "I think the Internet will open up a private practice to the world," Luciani says. "Psychologists will become more involved in online promotions and Skype sessions. Blogging, podcasts, etc. are the advent of this future."[23]

And as society in general becomes more aware of how common mental disorders are and of the adverse health impacts of stress, the need for trained professionals in our personal lives, at school and at work, has never been greater.

Find Out More

American Psychology Association (APA)
750 First St. NE
Washington, DC 20002
website: www.apa.org

The APA's website includes a "Careers" section that starts with the basics, describing the field of psychology and the range of psychologist jobs one can pursue. You can learn about where the jobs are, how much they pay, and what kind of education it takes to get there.

Careers in Psychology
website: https://careersinpsychology.org

Learn more about the varied career paths in psychology, what to look for in a university program, and how experts in the field started out and moved along their own paths. This website also contains articles about mental health breakthroughs and conditions.

Pursuing Psychology Careers Page
website: https://sites.uni.edu/walsh/linda1.html

On this web page, University of Northern Iowa psychology professor Linda Walsh has assembled dozens of links related to earning a psychology degree, job descriptions, and how to make the most of your psychology education.

Cybersecurity Expert

What Does a Cybersecurity Expert Do?

Cybersecurity is the protection of computer systems connected to the Internet, involving both the hardware and the software. Cybersecurity experts, also known as information security analysts, plan and execute measures to protect an organization's computer systems and networks. Their job is not only to respond quickly to hacks and other attacks on the system but also to anticipate future aggression and try to stay one step ahead of spies, thieves, or anyone else wanting to steal information or harm someone's computer systems, says Li-Chiou Chen, a professor at the Seidenberg School of Computer Science and Information Systems at Pace University in New York. "A cybersecurity consultant can help companies determine what methods should be used to secure their systems, to discover vulnerabilities in the systems, to develop security policies to reduce their risks, or to prepare the companies for regulatory compliance,"[24] she says.

Cybersecurity experts work with the latest in technology and are often privy to industry secrets and classified government information that must be protected. They keep up with the latest in computer security measures as well as the newest approaches that cyberthieves and spies use to get past those security walls, passwords, and other defenses.

A Typical Workday

Cybersecurity experts spend part of each workday monitoring computer systems and reviewing security reports about new threats or attacks elsewhere. Monitoring a computer system involves, among other tasks, running management software programs that send out alerts when anything unusual is discovered and then responding to those alerts if needed.

The job also demands that a cybersecurity professional look for weaknesses in a system, which can mean staging a mock cyberattack to test security measures that are already in place. The results of such tests can lead a cybersecurity professional to write new code, install software, or make other changes to bolster a system's defenses.

A typical workday can also include a response to an actual cyberattack. Once alerted to trouble, a cybersecurity expert will identify the attack, isolate the affected part of the system so no further damage can be done, address any weak spots, alert clients and other users to the status of the system, and implement steps to prevent more harm to the system. Responding to an attack can require hours of extra work, meaning that a so-called typical workday can extend late into the night on occasion.

Education and Training

A bachelor's degree in a computer-related field is generally required to start a career in cybersecurity. Many colleges and universities now offer actual cybersecurity degrees. Yet Sean Tierney, head of the cyberintelligence team at Infoblox, a security and automation company in California, suggests that studying aspects of computer science other than cybersecurity can be helpful because it makes you a specialist in an area that is still affected by

A Career for the Curious

"I've always liked finding loopholes in rules and such to the dismay of my teachers sometimes. I love knowing the details of how things work. Cybersecurity is a really good combination of the two once you really get into it."

—Sophia Anderson, a Willamette University student and member of the school's competitive Student (Cyber) Security League

Quoted in Willamette University, "Students Learn Cybersecurity Skills for Competition and Careers," February 12, 2019. http://willamette.edu.

cybersecurity. "The thing that will make you good at security is that you are great at something else first," he says. "For example, become a master of the fundamentals of data networks, be an expert at administering multiple operating systems or be proficient at multiple scripting languages."[25]

Internships with the cybersecurity divisions of companies or government agencies can offer valuable experience while you're in school. Ongoing training once you're in the workforce is also essential, as computer technology changes rapidly and developments in cybersecurity and cyberattacks are also changing constantly. "Cybersecurity professionals need to stay abreast of changes in the technology landscape and make continuous education a habit," says Michael Figueroa, the executive director of the Advanced Cyber Security Center in Bedford, Massachusetts. "They can easily do that by joining local information-sharing or other interest groups and attending security conferences."[26]

Skills and Personality

Clearly, computer skills are at the top of the list of qualities a cybersecurity expert needs. But the desire to work with the latest tools must be accompanied by integrity and a commitment to helping thwart crime and harm. "Similar to other jobs in the industry, cybersecurity professionals need to be a team player and communicate well," Chen says. "Most importantly, these professionals need to have computer ethics and be aware of security-related policies and laws. Cyberspace connects different aspects of our life these days. It is evolving, and it needs everyone's involvement to keep it a nice place."[27]

Cybersecurity experts often work with clients or others who have significantly less computer knowledge. Therefore, to harden a system's defenses, security analysts need to be able to patiently explain what is needed and why. In some cases, this requires the ability to translate highly technical language into words and concepts nonexperts can understand. You may at times work as part of a team of people who each bring a certain expertise to the job. Specialties in cybersecurity include data loss prevention, secure software development, and forensic analysis, among others.

Cyberattacks are serious problems in an environment that requires solutions to be quickly and thoroughly implemented. This means cybersecurity experts must be able to think quickly and calmly during a crisis. Being able to solve problems when time is working against you is at the very core of what being a cybersecurity expert is all about.

Working Conditions

Nearly every industry, organization, and governmental body relies on the Internet and a wide array of computer technology. So, cybersecurity experts are employed in banks, corporations, universities, government agencies, and many other organizations. Most of the work is done indoors at a computer. Cybersecurity consultants may have their own offices from which they can monitor and respond to various threats or emergencies. Travel to a client's location or to the sites of computer systems under your watch may also be required if a problem can't be solved remotely or if there was physical harm done to a computer system.

Employers and Pay

Cybersecurity experts work for the government as well as for the private sector, either as consultants hired by companies to provide security services or as employees of corporations in their information technology divisions. Cybersecurity consulting firms typically have multiple clients for whom they provide services. Governments at all levels have cybersecurity experts protecting systems related to everything from voter rolls to top secret military information.

Although the median pay for an information security analyst is $95,510, the job can pay well into six figures, particularly if you're working in the private sector. Banks and other financial institutions pay an average of $108,000, while tech companies pay more than $110,000 on average. But for cybersecurity experts who want to work for the federal government, good pay isn't the only motivator. Lee Vorthman, the chief technology officer with NetApp's federal civilian agencies unit, says that cybersecurity experts tend to remain longer with their employers than many other people working in tech. NetApp is a California cloud data services and data management company. "These people aren't jumping from job to job looking for salary bumps and signing bonuses," he says. "Many of them want to work for federal agencies and most of them tend to stick with employers for the long term. For companies, that means they better get them early or risk not getting them at all."[28]

What Is the Future Outlook for Cybersecurity Experts?

The increasing threat of cybercrimes and cyberattacks on public and private computer systems is alarming. However, it does mean that the need for qualified cybersecurity experts is also on the rise. According to Charles Cadenhead, who teaches networking and computer support at Brookhaven College in Texas,

> We always need networking professionals. Right now, there are more jobs than there are people training in security. We've seen [the number of students in] our security classes go up. The more dependent we become on computers, the more we need security experts.[29]

The growth in this career path is likely to exceed that of most other professions, partly because the threat of cyberattacks continues to rise. Local, state, and federal government agencies in particular will spend the next several years recruiting and training the next generation of cybersecurity experts for a wide range of responsibilities.

Willamette University associate professor of computer science Fritz Ruehr, adviser to the college's Student (Cyber) Security League, recalled learning about a cybersecurity conference sponsored by the federal government. Instead of charging attendees to the conference a fee, the government was ready to pay $1,000 to each person interested in learning more about cybersecurity career options at the federal level. "It was very clear that at the federal level, they were willing to spend millions because they are scared witless," Ruehr said. "At the workshop, they spent several hours convincing us that cybersecurity is a huge national issue that could go wrong at any moment in a horrifying way."[30] The more information that is stored and transmitted through the Internet, the more important it will be to have trained, talented cybersecurity experts to keep that data safe.

Find Out More

CyberCareers.gov
website: www.cybercareers.gov

Operated by the US Office of Personnel Management, this federal government site profiles people who work in cybersecurity, lists benefits relating to the career field, and includes information about current job openings with the government and why a career in cybersecurity can be an exciting career choice.

Cyber Security Education
website: www.cybersecurityeducation.org/careers

This site takes you through several of the main career paths in cybersecurity, including cryptographer, vulnerability assessor, forensic expert, and security engineer. You can learn how each of these fields and others differ and what experience and training you'll need for each path.

National Cyber League
5910 Connecticut Ave., #15522
Chevy Chase, MD 20825
website: www.nationalcyberleague.org

This organization sponsors high school and college competitions in cybersecurity, mirroring the kinds of challenges you'll face on the job. There are opportunities for team and individual competitions. See what the cybergames are all about and maybe get a team together at your school.

Paramedic

A Few Facts

Number of Jobs
248,000 paramedics in
2016*

Median Salary
$33,380 in 2017*

**Minimum Educational
Requirements**
High school diploma

Certification and Licensing
National EMT Certification
and National Paramedic
Certification

Personal Qualities
Ability to assess a situation
quickly; resourcefulness;
good communication skills;
physically fit

Work Settings
At emergency scenes, both
indoors and outdoors, and in
moving ambulances

Future Job Outlook
15 percent growth through
2026*

* Numbers include paramedics and
  emergency medical technicians

What Does a Paramedic Do?

Few jobs require the kind of fast-paced problem-solving skills necessary to succeed as a paramedic. A paramedic provides emergency care on the spot to people who have been injured or who are suffering symptoms of a medical crisis, such as a heart attack or a drug overdose. The problem could be a severe injury or serious symptoms, such as unconsciousness, chest pains, or difficulty breathing. Solving the problem means rapidly assessing the key symptoms, determining their most likely causes, and then keeping the person alive and stable until a doctor can begin a more thorough treatment plan.

Paramedics usually arrive at the scene of an emergency following a 911 call. They are often the first ones there to help people in dire need. The first task of the paramedic is to assess the person's condition and determine the most immediate needs. "I just look at what happened and I try to put together a plan," says Colorado paramedic Nate Boyce. "And as soon as I have a plan for how I want to treat the patient, that's just what I do."[31]

A paramedic often performs lifesaving procedures at the scene prior to taking a patient to the emergency room. Some of this care includes treating a bleeding wound with a tourniquet or placing a tube down a person's throat to help him or her breathe—a procedure known as intubating. Other calls aren't life threatening but require a paramedic to evaluate a patient's condition, perform first aid, and get them to a hospital for further evaluation and treatment.

A paramedic must be prepared to treat all types of medical emergencies, such as burns, broken bones, deep lacerations, concussions, and many other injuries, as well as conditions such as heart attack, stroke, choking, and suspected poisoning. A pregnant woman who goes into labor suddenly may need a paramedic to deliver the baby. In such a situation, the paramedic must decide whether transportation to a hospital would be possible or would be too risky to the mother and child.

A Typical Workday

About the only consistent thing about a paramedic's workday is that every call they respond to will be different from the last. "It's different every time; there's no monotony to it," says Jason Hernandez, a paramedic in Fort Worth, Texas.

> Yesterday, for example, I had two patients with almost identical symptoms, but completely different problems. They were both having what appeared to be anxiety attacks, but one was, I believe, cholecystitis—gallstones. The other patient had a broken rib, but the symptoms were exactly the same.[32]

Like other first responders, paramedics work shifts that may have them on the job during the day or night. A shift usually begins with a paramedic collecting supplies at the hospital or fire station or wherever his or her ambulance is based. After making sure the ambulance is stocked with the medications and other supplies, a paramedic will then wait for that first call.

Paramedics usually work in pairs. The pairing may be two paramedics or one paramedic and one EMT. (EMTs, or emergency medical technicians, have less training and experience than a certified paramedic. However, many paramedics begin their careers as EMTs.) When they are called out to an emergency, paramedics are given information about the situation from the dispatcher. The person making the 911 call may be relating symptoms to the dispatcher so that the paramedics will have some idea about the nature of the emergency when they arrive on the scene. Paramedics are in touch with doctors and nurses at the hospital while treating patients at the scene, getting advice about medications and other treatments to help stabilize the patients. This is done with two-way radios or, in some situations, with video technology that allows a doctor at a hospital to see the patient and the injury, if there is one. This type of technology is especially helpful in rural areas, where paramedics have to treat patients many miles from the nearest hospital.

A major challenge for paramedics is that many conditions have similar symptoms. Some are signs of a life-threatening problem, but others are more benign. Responding to a patient complaining of chest pain is a frequent scenario for paramedics most days. Such symptoms could indicate a heart attack or other cardiac problem, such as an aneurysm. But chest pain can also be a sign of heartburn or a pulled muscle in the chest. "For chest pain, which is another really frequent [complaint], those are harder to diagnose," Hernandez says. "It could just be acid reflux, or a heart attack, or an asthma attack, or a blood clot in the lungs. There's no sure way of fully diagnosing it in the field. You've got to use all of your knowledge to figure out as best you can what they've got going on."[33]

After treating the patient at the scene, one paramedic or EMT will drive the ambulance while a paramedic will remain in the back tending to the patient. Once at the emergency department of a hospital, the paramedics will make sure the patient is safely under the care of hospital nurses and doctors.

Paramedics must complete a report about each call to which they respond, listing all pertinent information about the patient, the nature of the emergency, and what treatment they provided. This information becomes part of a patient's medical file, and it helps physicians track changes in blood pressure, heart rate, and other symptoms. Detailed records are also important to the hospital and health insurance provider, who want careful record keeping of all medications and treatments that were provided to the insured. Patients or their insurance company are billed for all treatments, so paramedics must keep track of everything that happens from the moment they arrive at the scene.

Education and Training

Paramedics must be at least eighteen years old and have a high school diploma. They also must be certified by the National Registry of Emergency Medical Technicians before they can become certified paramedics. Their training includes classroom studies of anatomy and biology and advanced life support training. Paramedics also study advanced cardiac care, patient stabilization and airway treatments, and other advanced emergency medical techniques. Much of this training and course work can be obtained at a community college.

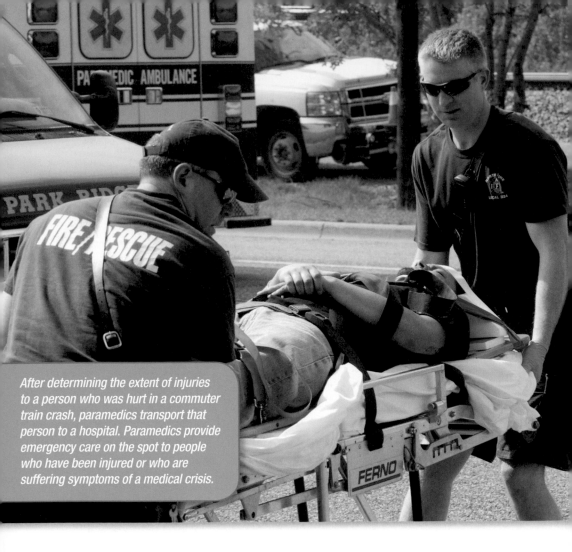

After determining the extent of injuries to a person who was hurt in a commuter train crash, paramedics transport that person to a hospital. Paramedics provide emergency care on the spot to people who have been injured or who are suffering symptoms of a medical crisis.

In order to earn National Paramedic Certification, a candidate must complete the course work and training, and then pass a written test about emergency medical care as well as a hands-on test responding to a medical trauma on a simulated patient. Nationally certified paramedics must also obtain a state license to work as a paramedic. Paramedics considering medical school or careers as clinical supervisors or health care administrators often earn four-year undergraduate degrees.

Skills and Personality

Paramedics can find themselves at the scene of horrific accidents, where injuries to one or more victims can be severe—even deadly. So, you need a strong stomach and the ability to handle traumatic medical emergencies with cool and calm. It's also vital that you can think on your feet, size up a crisis in a hurry, and come up with a logical treatment based on your observations and experience.

Working Conditions

The job may take paramedics outdoors or indoors, wherever people are injured or experience a medical emergency. That can mean helping people in rainy weather, heat waves, or snow-storms. Depending on whether paramedics work in a city or a more rural area, they may be providing services on crowded streets or out in the country, far from a hospital. Paramedics are also on hand at events with large crowds, where an injury or sudden event, such as a heart attack, may occur. Paramedics often work twelve-hour shifts, sometimes grabbing a little sleep when they can. In some departments, shifts are eight hours, but others are twenty-four hours, with forty-eight hours off in between those longer shifts. Paramedics usually operate out of fire stations or hospitals, and they often work alongside fire-fighters when responding to traffic accidents, fires, and other emergencies.

Employers and Pay

Most paramedics work for the emergency medical services (EMS) department of a city or county. They are government employees, so their raises tend to follow a schedule that is approved by a city council, county commission, or other governmental agency, and their salaries are negotiated in many regions by a labor union. Some communities use a combination of public and private am-bulance and paramedic services. Private paramedic services in these areas generally respond to less severe, non-life-threatening emergencies.

More than First Aid

"EMS is not what a person sees on TV with rushing lights and sirens after major car accidents and traumatic injuries. EMS is holding the hand of the elderly female who just lost her husband; the 2 a.m. calls because someone is sick or scared and not sure what to do. It takes a very compassionate person with quick thinking to work in EMS along with a desire to always keep learning."

—Kayla Franck, a paramedic in Spokane, Washington

Quoted in INHS Health Training, "Kayla Found Her EMS Career." https://healthtraining.inhs.org.

The median pay for a paramedic is $33,380, but salaries vary widely based on the cost of living in a particular community and the demands on the EMS department. The median salary as a paramedic for a city or county would be closer to $40,000, while a paramedic for a private ambulance service might make closer to $33,000. A busy EMS department in a large city will pay more than one in a more rural area with fewer demands on the paramedics.

What Is the Future Outlook for Paramedics?

Because paramedics are solving life-and-death problems in high-pressure situations, the job is not for everyone. That means that people who are willing to go through the training and deal with the challenges of the job should be able to find jobs now and well into the future. "Most jurisdictions are short on paramedics, so we are very much in demand,"[34] says Dan Jones, a paramedic instructor with Carroll Community College in Maryland.

The expected job growth for paramedics is about 15 percent. Fueling that growth, in part, is the aging of America. As the percentage of elder Americans grows, there are greater demands on all aspects of health care, including emergency responders.

Find Out More

EMS1

website: www.ems1.com

This site includes the latest news involving paramedics from around the country and offers information about training requirements and career opportunities. You can read articles or watch videos all relating to the education, training, and job of paramedics.

National Registry of Emergency Medical Technicians

6610 Busch Blvd.
Columbus, OH 43229
website: www.nremt.org

This site is sponsored by the organization that certifies paramedics and EMTs. It includes information on education requirements and types of exams needed for paramedic certification, ways to volunteer, state-specific licensing requirements, and other aspects of the job.

Wisconsin Health Careers

website: https://wihealthcareers.org

This University of Wisconsin site explains a step-by-step approach to becoming a paramedic, including recommended high school classes and the tests needed to actually earn EMT certification. It also includes a list of professional organizations that can provide more information about a range of health care careers.

School Administrator

A Few Facts

Number of Jobs
244,690

Median Salary
$97,640 in 2017

Minimum Educational Requirements
Master's degree

Personal Qualities
Good at organizing, planning, and problem solving; detail oriented; comfortable communicating with a variety of people; service oriented

Work Settings
Public or private schools, from preschool through high school

Future Job Outlook
8 percent growth through 2026

What Does a School Administrator Do?

Whether it's running a small private preschool or a huge public high school, the job of school administrator requires problem-solving skills that range from mediating minor student conflicts to stretching limited financial resources to meet the needs of teachers and kids. A school administrator can be a principal or an assistant principal. Some schools also use the term *vice principal* or *dean* when describing the administrator who works just below the principal.

A school principal oversees all aspects of school operations. This includes curriculum, staffing, professional development of all staff members, maintenance of the buildings and campus grounds, budgets, food service, interacting with parents and others in the community, and doing what it takes to provide a safe and effective environment for student learning. Other administrators, such as assistant principals, may focus on issues such as student discipline, teacher evaluations, and scheduling. All of the responsibilities facing school administrators present an ongoing and wide-ranging series of financial, logistical, and educational problems, and underlying all the various solutions should be a focus on what's best for the students.

School administrators apply their problem-solving skills daily as they help students, teachers, and others in the school community meet or exceed their goals. To get everyone there, administrators spend a lot of time in meetings, brainstorming sessions, and collaborative work with educators within the school and with other administrators at the school district level, such as the superintendent and various district department heads. "Ensuring the safety of students and faculty is my primary responsibility and equally important as continuing to develop and improve student learning opportunities through the latest research,"[35] says Scott Crisp, the principal of Jackson Hole High School in Wyoming.

Sometimes, school administrators look for ways to solve problems even before they become apparent. The most effective problem solvers can spot trouble ahead of time and devise solutions that prevent issues down the road. Creative and effective school administrators often have to get resourceful and try programs that aren't part of a traditional school experience. Jennifer Hogan, an assistant principal at Hoover High School in Alabama, launched a program to make sure every student had a "go-to" teacher or other adult in the school who could serve as a mentor, advocate, or just a supportive listener. She hung pictures of all returning students in a conference room and asked teachers to choose students with whom they had a positive relationship. Any students not selected were placed on a list, and teachers were encouraged to "adopt" students to make sure that everyone had someone looking out for them. "We want all students to have a sense of belonging and know that they are cared for, and this activity helped our staff ensure that all students had an advocate,"[36] Hogan says.

A Typical Workday

School administrators usually have an early start to their day, arriving before the students each morning. Many school administrators like to be visible on campus, greeting students as they arrive and teachers as they go to their classrooms. Then it's a full day of work that usually lasts well after the students leave campus.

Some days can provide a little fun, like honoring the school's teacher of the year or participating in a school's spirit week or homecoming activities. Other responsibilities can be much more serious and can test an administrator's problem-solving abilities. For example, a fight between students that took place over the weekend can spill into Monday morning, requiring the efforts of the school administrator to cool things off between the kids and keep the conflict from continuing or drawing in other students. Or an administrator at a school where student test scores aren't meeting expectations will meet with teachers or district personnel to work out strategies for improving student performance. Principals also spend time regularly working on professional development programs, which are designed to make teachers and administrators more effective in their jobs.

Crisp says the many demands of being a school administrator require that you be able to solve problems in the moment while also considering the long-term implications of your decisions. But an administrator can't forget that the whole purpose of school is to educate young minds. As Crisp says,

> The day of the principal can be both predictable and chaotic. My role requires the ability to situationally pivot on the fly in order to meet the immediate needs of students, parents, faculty, and other stakeholders. I must be sensitive to a variety of immediate and long-term demands, while simultaneously balancing the interests and beliefs of the school community. However, regardless of the complexity, keeping student achievement at the core of the work can act as a grounding mechanism to assist in decision making and doing what is best for students.[37]

Education and Training

Most school administrators have at least a master's degree. The graduate degree is often in education administration or a related field, such as elementary education, secondary education (for high school teachers and administrators), or curriculum and instruction. Many assistant principals, principals, and school district administrators, such as superintendents or department heads, have doctoral degrees.

Many school administrators start their careers as classroom teachers. They make the move into administration as assistant principals, having earned a master's degree and having completed other types of training, such as workshops on educational leadership. While principals make sure their teachers and administrators complete professional development training, the principals themselves participate in similar programs to improve their leadership abilities and to keep up with the latest education research.

A high school administrator chats with students on campus. School administrators have a range of responsibilities, including overseeing school finances and policies and working directly with students, teachers, and parents.

Skills and Personality

A school administrator should be a good public speaker and comfortable talking with students and adults alike. Versatility and the ability to quickly move from one responsibility to another can't be overstated. One minute you're hiring an art teacher and the next you're at the school district headquarters learning about next year's budget and new testing requirements.

Because children's lives and futures are in the hands of educators, school administrators need to be courageous and always be searching for solutions to societal problems that impact students. Sanée Bell, a middle school principal in Houston, Texas, says one of the biggest problems school administrators face is helping students who are too often left behind or marginalized because of race, socioeconomic status, disabilities, or other reasons. According to Bell,

Inequity is robbing students of the best experiences they will never have if we are not courageous about addressing the inequity we see in public education. Even if we have students or teachers who don't believe, we must always believe in the possibility and potential of every teacher and every student. As the leader, we have to carry the torch and find a way. . . . Being courageous and hopeful won't amount to anything if we don't move beyond the conversation. We must put feet to our words by developing plans that intentionally challenge, address, and eradicate inequity.[38]

Working Conditions

A classroom teacher typically works 187 days per year, though summer breaks are often filled with course work toward an advanced degree or training and preparing for the next school year. A school administrator often works more than 220 days per year. A middle or high school principal may have a slightly longer contract than an elementary school principal. When students are off school for the summer, an administrator may be working on hiring new teachers and staff for the upcoming school year or overseeing renovations or other changes on campus.

An administrator often spends part of the day in an office and the rest of the day elsewhere on campus, monitoring lunchtime in the cafeteria, visiting classrooms, or meeting with colleagues. Working in school administration means working with a team to solve problems, and that can be some of the most rewarding parts of the job. Sue Astley, the principal of St. Martin's Episcopal School in Atlanta, Georgia, acknowledges the fun of interacting with fellow administrators and teachers, "especially when we're problem solving or discussing some new, innovative ideas that they want to put to use in the classroom."[39]

Employers and Pay

School administrators who work in public education are employed by school districts. They report to the district's superintendent, who in turn answers to the district's school board. A principal usually has the final say on hiring assistant principals and others on a school's staff. School districts typically have a pay range for administrators at the high school, middle school, and elementary school levels. In part because they are contracted to work more days per year, high school administrators are paid more than elementary school and middle school administrators. The average salary for an elementary school principal is about $92,000, while a high school principal makes, on average, about $104,000.

Private schools usually have a board of directors or a similar body that oversees the hiring and firing of administrators. Depending on who operates the private school and how prestigious it is, the pay may be more or less than what a comparable job pays in the public school system.

What Is the Future Outlook for School Administrators?

The demand for school administrators is expected to grow about 8 percent through 2026. Issues such as merit pay for teachers based on student test scores, online classes, and a student body that is getting more diverse around the country will continue to be hot topics for school administrators. All of these issues may present opportunities to transform schools and the delivery of education, but they will also present new sets of problems for principals and assistant principals to solve.

Find Out More

Education Connection

website: www.educationconnection.com/online-degrees/how-to
-become-a-principal

In the "How to Become a Principal" section of this website, you can learn about the differences between being an elementary and secondary school principal as well as how the various education degrees can help prepare you for a range of jobs in school administration.

Northeastern University Graduate Programs Blog

website: www.northeastern.edu/graduate/blog

Whether you want to be a principal, superintendent, curriculum director, or other school administrator, this blog's "7 Careers to Consider in Education Administration" post provides helpful information about each job's responsibilities, job prospects, and salaries.

Teacher.org

website: www.teacher.org

On this site, you can learn about the qualities it takes to be a good principal in the "How to Become a Principal" section. It outlines the job duties of a school's top administrator and provides links to many university programs in education administration.

Law Enforcement Officer

A Few Facts

Number of Jobs
807,000 in 2016

Median Salary
$62,960

Minimum Educational Requirements
At least a high school diploma

Certification and Licensing
Graduation from a law enforcement agency's academy; state-issued law enforcement officer certification

Personal Qualities
Confidence; empathy; negotiating skills; problem-solving ability; communication skills; physical and mental fitness; integrity

Work Settings
Both indoors and outdoors in many locations in the community, including some dangerous places

Future Job Outlook
7 percent growth through 2026

What Does a Law Enforcement Officer Do?

The motto To Serve and Protect pretty much sums up the job of a law enforcement officer. Police officers, sheriff's deputies, and others in law enforcement serve the public and pledge to protect people and property.

In so doing, law enforcement officers spend most of their time solving problems or trying to prevent problems from developing in the first place. Crime prevention is the focus of any successful law enforcement agency, says William Bratton, who served as the police commissioner for both Boston and New York and was also the chief of the Los Angeles Police Department. "Too often police departments tried to arrest their way out of problems, but that does not work," Bratton says. "We need to continue learning, collaborating and partnering. The three P's are most important to good police work—partnerships, problem solving and prevention."[40]

The specific duties of law enforcement officers vary depending on their rank and their unit within the agency. Patrol officers spend much of their day in an assigned patrol area, looking for signs of trouble, responding to emergencies, and getting to know the people who live and work in that area. Patrols may take place in a car, on foot, on a bicycle, or even on horseback in some communities. Detectives investigate crimes after they have been reported, searching for suspects, gathering evidence, and assisting prosecutors.

In addition to traditional law enforcement agencies employed by a city or county, there are state law enforcement officers who patrol the highways, federal border patrol agents, Secret Service agents who protect the president and other top federal officials, federal Drug Enforcement Agency officers, and other jobs that still fall under the law enforcement designation. Each branch of the military has its own police force. Military police officers patrol, enforce laws, and investigate crimes on military installations around the world. Some patrol officers choose to work as school resource officers, providing campus security and teaching students about issues such as gangs and drugs.

But local police officers and sheriff's deputies still make up the bulk of law enforcement occupations. And the demands on them continue to grow, requiring ever more sophisticated problem-solving skills. "The role of a police officer has drastically expanded over the years," said Portage, Illinois, police chief Troy Williams.

> They are asked to be a counselor, a healer, a mentor, a temporary parent, a voice of reason, the clergy, technically savvy, solve crimes, keep schools secure, make arrests and so much more. And they are expected to do all this without emotion, judgment or feelings.[41]

A Typical Workday

The average workday for a patrol officer is markedly different from that of a detective working on a murder investigation or other serious crime. Detectives spend their days interviewing witnesses or others who may have useful information. They gather evidence and work with evidence technicians and crime lab technicians to learn more about the crime scene and anyone who may have been involved. They analyze information, such as fingerprints and security camera footage; get information about cars based on license plate numbers; and follow up on leads they get from witnesses or anonymous tips.

Patrol officers, on the other hand, start their days by attending a roll call at a station, at which time they are given updates about possible crimes or other activities in the community. Then they start patrolling the zone to which they are assigned. They may give out traffic citations or warnings part of the day while also dropping in on local businesses to talk about security and about any changes in the area they have noticed. Police officers also meet with homeowner groups to talk about better neighborhood lighting or other crime-prevention strategies. And, of course, police officers often get dispatched to respond to calls for help, related either to a crime that has been reported or to someone in need of assistance, such as a motorist with a car that has stalled in the middle of a busy street or a parent whose child has wandered off. Many calls to the police are from people who have been victims of a crime, such as a break-in at their home or a sexual assault.

"There is no such thing as a routine day in the life of a police officer," says David Stevens, a veteran of the Jacksonville Police Department in Florida. "Even what is considered a simple traffic stop is not simple because you never know who is behind the wheel."[42] The unpredictability makes the job endlessly interesting, but it also causes officers to be especially careful on the job, he adds.

Education and Training

Entry-level jobs in law enforcement require at least a high school diploma and graduation from an agency's training academy, where recruits learn firearms, investigative procedures, criminal law, leadership, physical fitness, and more. To advance into supervisory roles, a college degree may be necessary, depending on the size of the department. To become a police chief or sheriff,

Cops in the Community

"I'm not convinced that walking beats, or police on bikes, or having police attend community meetings are sufficient commitment to community policing. Something deeper is needed. I am committed to the notion that problem solving is a core component of all effective community policing efforts, not a sideline."

—Sean Varano, a professor of criminal justice at Roger Williams University in Rhode Island

Sean Varano, "When Police Are Problem Solvers," LISC, March 22, 2017. www.lisc.org.

or even a higher-ranking officer, an associate's degree or bachelor's degree is usually required, along with years of service. A master's degree in law enforcement leadership or a related field may be helpful to advance more quickly to a higher rank.

Law enforcement officers also participate in ongoing training in areas such as firearms; leadership; tactics; and changes in federal, state, or local laws that might impact policing. An officer may choose to work with the K-9 unit that employs dogs to help with tasks such as apprehending suspects; tracking missing people; detecting illegal drugs, explosives, or dangerous chemicals; and helping calm children and other people during a crisis.

Skills and Personality

Being able to keep a cool head in a crisis is one of the most important traits of any law enforcement officer. You need to be able to size up a situation quickly and solve the problem at hand. The challenge could be breaking up a fight and figuring out who—if anyone—should be charged with a crime, responding to a neighbor's complaint about a noisy party, or helping a person who may be mentally ill and wandering the streets. Sometimes problem solving requires force, but most of the time it's a matter of talking calmly with people, de-escalating tensions, separating people in a serious dispute, getting help from other agencies or from people in the community, or employing other nonaggressive strategies.

All Kinds of People

"What makes the job challenging is the different people we have to deal with on any given basis. Sometimes you are dealing with people that are on drugs, have mental problems, and might also be carrying weapons that are dangerous to other officers."

—Blaine Shutts, a police officer in Oskaloosa, Iowa

Quoted in Jonathan R. Pitman, "The Challenges of Being a Police Officer," *Oskaloosa Herald*, August 7, 2014. www.oskaloosa.com.

Speaking a second language is helpful in many locations. Given that millions of people in the United States report that they do not speak English well, having a law enforcement officer available who can ask questions and explain things in a person's native language can have a big impact on solving crimes and enhancing police relations in a community.

Working Conditions

The job of a law enforcement officer involves working in a wide variety of settings. It can mean working with a partner on the night shift in a big, bustling city or starting your day at dawn in a small town with low crime but a small police department. You can spend much of the day in a patrol car, at a desk, or in a crime lab, or you can be at a crime scene all day or night, gathering evidence, talking to witnesses, keeping onlookers away, and assisting detectives. Some police departments will assign junior officers to handle crowd control at outdoor events, such as concerts or athletic competitions. Such duties expose an officer to all sorts of weather, from extreme heat to bitter cold.

Employers and Pay

Cities, counties, and states employ law enforcement officers; these officers are government workers entitled to many of the same benefits as other civil servants. Law enforcement officers average $62,960 a year, but that salary varies widely, depending on an officer's rank and years of service as well as the area in which he or she works. A police officer in Chicago, for example, will make more than an officer of similar rank in a small town a hundred miles from Chicago. State troopers make, on average around $71,000 a year, while officers on a college campus police force may make closer to $54,000 annually.

What Is the Future Outlook for Law Enforcement Officers?

Though job growth looks steady in the years ahead, police departments and other agencies have been facing a shortage of men and women interested in pursuing careers in law enforcement. Issues surrounding gun rights, school violence, changing approaches to enforcing drug laws, and other matters that affect crime and public safety are making an already complicated job even more challenging.

But Corporal Jerry Patrick of the Dyer, Illinois, police department says that public service and the desire to help tackle problems in a community are still important to the next generation. "There is still a strong interest within our youth," he says. "No matter how hard or unpopular this job may become, I am very confident there will always be someone who will step up to take care of others. I am very proud of that fact."[43]

Find Out More
American Police Hall of Fame and Museum
6350 Horizon Dr.
Titusville, FL 32780
website: www.aphf.org

Check out the history of police work in the United States and explore the many programs online or in person at this unique museum and information center. Learn how crime labs operate and how high-tech tools are making their way into law enforcement work.

LawEnforcementEDU.net
website: www.lawenforcementedu.net

Learn the how-to's of becoming a law enforcement officer, including a police officer, a K-9 officer, or a homicide detective. You can also learn about the various ranks of police officers and sheriff's deputies.

Legal Career Path
website: https://legalcareerpath.com

Learn about the many kinds of law enforcement office jobs available, including uniformed officers, investigators, and support positions, as well as what it takes to start your law enforcement career.

Source Notes

Introduction: Making a Living Solving Problems

1. Quoted in Anuradha K. Herath, "Getting to Mars Means Stopping and Landing," *AstroBiology Magazine*, April 4, 2011. www.astrobio.net.

Biomedical Engineer

2. Quoted in Alliance for Advanced Biomedical Engineering, "Smart Stents Detect Narrowing Arteries," July 30, 2018. https://aabme.asme.org.
3. Quoted in Alissa Mallinson, February 3, 2015. "Ioannis Yannas to Be Inducted into the Inventors Hall of Fame," MIT News. http://news.mit.edu.
4. Quoted in Alexandrous Houssein, "Succeeding as a Woman in Biological Engineering," *BMC Series* (blog), January 9, 2019. http://blogs.biomedcentral.com.
5. Quoted in ScienceDaily, "Bioengineers Create Ultrasmall, Light-Activated Electrode for Neural Stimulation," February 15, 2019. www.sciencedaily.com.
6. Quoted in Kurt Schlosser, "Geek of the Week: Bioengineering PhD Shivani Keeps Learning in Search for Ideas at Xinova," *GeekWire*, October 12, 2018. www.geekwire.com.
7. Quoted in Kasey Panetta, "How This Biomedical Engineer Landed Her Dream Job," *ECN*, January 9, 2015. www.ecn mag.com.

Human Resources Manager

8. Quoted in Will Erstad, "11 Rewarding Reasons to Work in HR," Rasmussen College, October 23, 2017. www.rasmus sen.edu.

9. Quoted in Jess Fuhl, "Why I Love Working in HR," Sage People, February 11, 2019. www.sagepeople.com.

10. Quoted in JobShadow.com, "Interview with a Human Resources Director." http://jobshadow.com.

11. Quoted in Fuhl, "Why I Love Working in HR."

12. Quoted in Susan Hauser, "Costly Degrees in HR Could Be Wise Choice vs. Certification," *Workforce*, November 19, 2012. www.workforce.com.

13. Quoted in Forbes Human Resources Council, "14 Ways HR Professionals Can Solve Workplace Conflict Efficiently," *Forbes*, April 10, 2018. https://forbes.com.

Tech Support Specialist

14. Quoted in *U.S. News & World Report*, "What Is a Computer Support Specialist?" https://money.usnews.com.

15. Quoted in Emily Matzelle, "A Day in the Life of an IT Pro: Tier 1 Help Desk Specialist," CompTIA, May 19, 2017. https://certification.comptia.org.

16. Quoted in *Dallas Community Colleges Student Blog*, "Reboot Your Career with a Computer Support Specialist Associate Degree," December 4, 2017. http://blog.dcccd.edu.

17. Quoted in Matzelle, "A Day in the Life of an IT Pro."

18. Quoted in HDI and Robert Half Technology, *The Technical Support Center of the Future*, HDI, 2013. www.thinkhdi.com.

Clinical Psychologist

19. Quoted in Margarita Tartakovsky, "Therapists Spill: Why I Love Being a Clinician," PsychCentral, October 8, 2018. https://psychcentral.com.

20. Quoted in Careers in Psychology, "Dr. Joseph Luciani, Clinical Psychologist." https://careersinpsychology.org.

21. Quoted in Careers in Psychology, "Dr. Joseph Luciani, Clinical Psychologist."

22. Quoted in Amy Novotney, "Psychology Job Forecast: Partly Sunny," *gradPSYCH Magazine*, March 2011. www.apa.org.
23. Quoted in Careers in Psychology, "Dr. Joseph Luciani, Clinical Psychologist."

Cybersecurity Expert

24. Quoted in Vicki Salemi, "You May Not Have Heard of These IT Jobs, but Demand for Them Is Soaring," *New York Post*, September 23, 2018. https://nypost.com.
25. Quoted in Laurence Bradford, "How to Start a Lucrative Career in Cybersecurity," *Forbes*, February 27, 2017. www .forbes.com.
26. Quoted in Salemi, "You May Not Have Heard of These IT Jobs, but Demand for Them Is Soaring."
27. Quoted in Salemi, "You May Not Have Heard of These IT Jobs, but Demand for Them Is Soaring."
28. Quoted in Kenneth Corbin, "Cybersecurity Pros in High Demand, Highly Paid and Highly Selective," *CIO*, August 8, 2013. www.cio.com.
29. Quoted in *Dallas Community Colleges Student Blog*, "Reboot Your Career with a Computer Support Specialist Associate Degree."
30. Quoted in Willamette University, "Students Learn Cybersecurity Skills for Competition and Careers," February 12, 2019. http://willamette.edu.

Paramedic

31. Quoted in Zach Sokol, "What's It Like to Save Lives as a 25-Year-Old Paramedic?," Vice, October 22, 2016. www.vice .com.
32. Quoted in Bourree Lam, "The Siren's Call," *Atlantic*, August 25, 2016. www.theatlantic.com.
33. Quoted in Lam, "The Siren's Call."

34. Quoted in Jon Kelvey, "Paramedics in Demand, Instructors Say, and College Program Helps Prepare Them," *Carroll County Times*, May 11, 2018. www.carrollcountytimes.com.

School Administrator

35. Scott Crisp, "A Day in the Life of a Principal," *Homeroom* (blog), US Department of Education, October 30, 2017. https://blog.ed.gov.
36. Quoted in National Association of Assistant School Principals, "2018 National Assistant Principal of the Year Finalists." www.nassp.org.
37. Crisp, "A Day in the Life of a Principal."
38. Quoted in Larry Ferlazzo, "Response: Challenges Prinicipals Face & How to Respond to Them," *Education Week*, February 24, 2018. www.edweek.org.
39. Quoted in Education World, "Principals Reflect on the Best Parts of the Job." www.educationworld.com.

Law Enforcement Officer

40. Quoted in George Mauzy, "Former Police Chief Says Crime Prevention Is the Goal," *Compass*, April 2, 2012. www.ohio.edu/compass.
41. Quoted in Jerry Davich, "Veteran Police Officers Insist They Would Still Join Force Despite Today's Challenges," *Chicago Tribune*, May 17, 2018. www.chicagotribune.com.
42. Quoted in Kenneth Amaro, "No Day Is Typical for a Police Officer," First Coast News, March 10, 2016. www.firstcoastnews.com.
43. Quoted in Davich, "Veteran Police Officers Insist They Would Still Join Force Despite Today's Challenges."

Interview with a Human Resources Manager

Carl Moyer is the human resources (HR) director at Parr Lumber in Portland, Oregon. He has worked as the company's HR manager and then its director for a total of three years. He answered questions about his career by email.

Q: Why did you become a human resources manager?

A: For twenty years, every company I worked for had an HR department that made me crazy. Their service to internal customers was awful (if not dysfunctional), and when I had the opportunity to put my money where my mouth was, I jumped at it. I needed to see if I could solve it, or if I was just a complainer.

Q: How did your previous jobs and education help prepare you for this position?

A: For a decade I was in operations and *used* HR, and for a decade I was in training and worked *with* HR. So, I was familiar with the needs and functions of HR—but I had to learn the subject matter expertise part on the job. While working at Parr, I earned a master's degree in business administration. Working full-time and taking classes part-time was a challenge, but I learned a lot and it definitely made me a stronger candidate when I applied for this job.

Q: Can you describe your typical workday?

A: The typical HR job is firefighting. The phone rings and e-mail comes in from sixty managers and/or any of eight hundred employees with issues and needs for our help. Could be that an employee is not doing a good job, and the manager needs help in holding him accountable. Or, an employee is getting the runaround from the insurance company, and she needs us to help solve the billing problem. There are countless issues to help with all day, every day.

Q: What do you like most about your job?

A: The best part is helping people. HR is a job that truly can make a difference in people's lives. If we educate people about our benefits, they can save money or improve their families' lives in a way they didn't know was possible until we taught them. We help with big-picture business issues like lowering turnover, improving hiring, and utilizing resources better, thereby making significant contributions to the bottom line. Super fun!

Q: What do you like least about your job?

A: The firefighting metaphor is useful: successful fire departments spend more time preventing fires than fighting them. When we spend too much time solving problems instead of educating and preventing, our job gets harder and less satisfying.

Q: What personal qualities do you find most valuable for this type of work?

A: Patience, empathy, HR-specific knowledge, and understanding of the business you're working within.

Q: What advice do you have for students who might be interested in this career?

A: Learn the business side of the work. How does the company make money? What do the majority of people do all day? You're going to be more successful if you understand those details. And you'll get more freedom in which to work if what you do affects the business in a real way. An HR department that shuffles paperwork and tries to enforce processes all day will not be a fun job—or that successful. But get involved in making your customers' lives better, and you'll get the keys to the kingdom—and have a great time doing it.

Other Careers If You Like Problem Solving

Actuary
Appliance repair
Archaeologist
Architect
Auto mechanic
Chief executive
Civil engineer
Computer engineer
Computer systems analyst
Economist
Emergency medical
  technician
Environmental engineer
Epidemiologist
Firefighter
Forensic scientist
Hospitalist

Judge
Lawyer
Mathematician
Mechanical engineer
Mediator
Midwife
Military officer
Nurse
Obstetrician
Ophthalmologist
Orthodontist
Physical therapist
Physician assistant
Physicist
Social worker
Surgeon
Veterinarian

Editor's note: The online *Occupational Outlook Handbook* of the US Department of Labor's Bureau of Labor Statistics is an excellent source of information on jobs in hundreds of career fields, including many of those listed here. The *Occupational Outlook Handbook* may be accessed online at www.bls.gov/ooh.

Index

Picture Credits

About the Author

James Roland started out as a newspaper reporter more than twenty-five years ago. He then moved on to become an editor, magazine writer, and author.